# Harley-Davidson

*Classic Motorcycles*
*1903–2006*

Fredric Winkowski
Jon Lopez

*additional photography by*
*Frank D. Sullivan*

This is a Parragon Publishing Book
First published in 2006
Conceived and produced by Glitterati Incorporated/www.glitteratiincorporated.com

Parragon Publishing
Queen Street House
4 Queen Street
Bath BA1 1HE, UK

ISBN 1-40547-593-5.

# Contents

# Introduction

*While William, Walter, and Arthur Davidson; William Harley; and their friend Ollie Evinrude may have hoped to one day convert their hobby into a business, it's safe to say that none of them could have foreseen the success story that their early venture has become. For more than a century, Harley-Davidson has been producing motorcycles of power, performance, and quality. The names of their products have become household words: Flathead, Panhead, Shovelhead, Knucklehead, Wide Glide, and Softail. Its products are iconic things of beauty that have defined the American experience. The company's success has given rise to a culture of bikers, known for free spirits and a love of the open road. To tell this story, we've selected vintage bikes; some are restored, others are not. There are also sport and touring bikes, daily-riders, choppers, and custom bikes shown here that are masterpieces of art in motion. There are also racers that have been so much a part of the American motor scene. The motorcycles in this collection are all significant additions to the Harley legend. Here in total is a visual history that showcases the bikes that are a part of the American adventure.*

# The History of Harley-Davidson

It was the dawn of the 20th century, and a feeling of dynamic optimism was in the air. In 1903, a group of friends who had blueprinted and built a new engine and mounted it in a frame of their design now offered it for sale as a Harley-Davidson motorcycle. The machine was built as a racer in a shed behind the family house. There were, of course, earlier attempts to add power to what were essentially bicycles; but these were unreliable, heavy Rube Goldberg contraptions destined for failure before they started.

Harley and Davidson realized that the internal combustion gas engine was the answer. To be a viable form of daily transportation on the roads of the day, which were largely unpaved, the motorcycle had to be ruggedly built, with a motor practical in design and construction. In early sales, Harley-Davidson sold 50 bikes in 1906, and was up to 1,100 by 1909. By then, work had shifted to a new plant on Chestnut Street in Milwaukee, Wisconsin, and the first V-twin came out the factory doors. By 1919, Harley-Davidson was second behind Indian with sales of 23,000 units a year, but the biggest competitor was the automobile in terms of price and comfort. To stay ahead, Harley realized that an on-going series of improvements was key, and their products reflected this thinking.

A chain drive replaced the leather belt, the sprung fork made the suspension more forgiving, and a three-speed transmission and an electric light made the first machines more useable, under all but the most trying conditions. Earlier, the bar-and-shield logo had appeared at the Patent office, and hill climb and dirt track racing were being used as important promotional tools to keep Harley in the public eye. During World War I the company had supplied 20,000 units to the Allies, the number of employees had jumped to 1,500, and their motorcycles were being exported to Japan. Fast and dependable, a Harley was ridden by Corporal Roy Holtz, the first American to enter Germany after the Armistice. In 1919 the Sport, with a directly opposed flat head configuration, was added to the line. The policy of gradual, evolutionary changes to their products coupled with a great business sense found the company with worldwide dealerships in 67 countries. In the US, a strong advertising and promotional budget supported sales, and a new dealership credit-program for their customers provided the public with even more incentive to purchase a motorcycle.

In 1913, the Racing Department was formed. In 1920, at the conclusion of a successful race, Leslie "Red" Parkhurst did a victory lap with the team mascot, a tiny pig, in his lap and started the "Hog" tradition. In 1922, the first 1213 cc V-twin was produced for the JD and FD models, and in 1925 the hallmark teardrop-shaped gas tank appeared. The second half of the roaring twenties provided the bike-buying public with several single-cylinder motorcycles-Models A, AA, B, and BA-and the first two-cam engine appeared on the JD series. Front wheel brakes are available, and the reliable 738 cc side-valve flathead V-twin appeared on the Model D.

One of the keys to Harley's success was that the company explored every market niche for a product that would fulfill a demand, all the while improving their existing product and technology. The Wall Street crash of 1929 and the Great

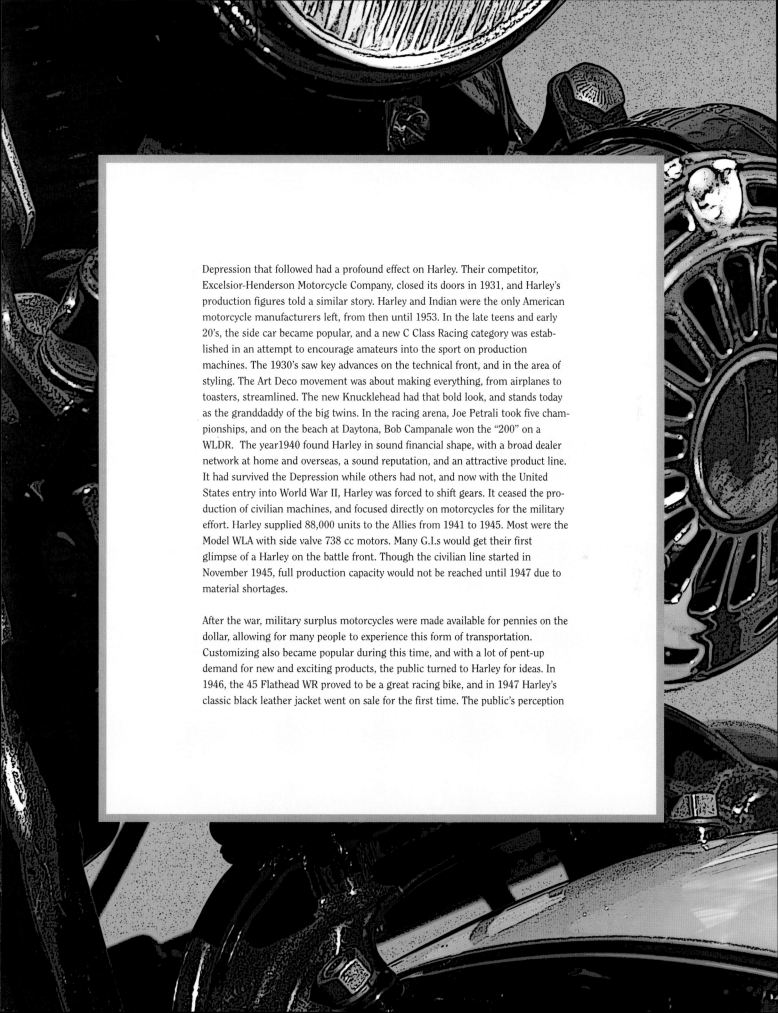

Depression that followed had a profound effect on Harley. Their competitor, Excelsior-Henderson Motorcycle Company, closed its doors in 1931, and Harley's production figures told a similar story. Harley and Indian were the only American motorcycle manufacturers left, from then until 1953. In the late teens and early 20's, the side car became popular, and a new C Class Racing category was established in an attempt to encourage amateurs into the sport on production machines. The 1930's saw key advances on the technical front, and in the area of styling. The Art Deco movement was about making everything, from airplanes to toasters, streamlined. The new Knucklehead had that bold look, and stands today as the granddaddy of the big twins. In the racing arena, Joe Petrali took five championships, and on the beach at Daytona, Bob Campanale won the "200" on a WLDR. The year1940 found Harley in sound financial shape, with a broad dealer network at home and overseas, a sound reputation, and an attractive product line. It had survived the Depression while others had not, and now with the United States entry into World War II, Harley was forced to shift gears. It ceased the production of civilian machines, and focused directly on motorcycles for the military effort. Harley supplied 88,000 units to the Allies from 1941 to 1945. Most were the Model WLA with side valve 738 cc motors. Many G.I.s would get their first glimpse of a Harley on the battle front. Though the civilian line started in November 1945, full production capacity would not be reached until 1947 due to material shortages.

After the war, military surplus motorcycles were made available for pennies on the dollar, allowing for many people to experience this form of transportation. Customizing also became popular during this time, and with a lot of pent-up demand for new and exciting products, the public turned to Harley for ideas. In 1946, the 45 Flathead WR proved to be a great racing bike, and in 1947 Harley's classic black leather jacket went on sale for the first time. The public's perception of motorcyclists had also changed, due partly to the bad publicity given to the biker gangs. In 1948, as part of the War Reparations Act, Harley acquired the 125 cc, lightweight, two-stroke DKW motorcycle from Germany, which found strong sales. That same year the Panhead, an update of the powerful Knucklehead, appeared with 1000 cc and 1213 cc of displacement, overhead valve engines, aluminum heads, hydraulic valve lifters, and chromed "cake pan" rocker covers. Hydraulic front forks on new models announced the Hydra Glide. In the meantime lighter, nimbler motorcycles from Great Britain threatened Harley's big twin position in price and performance. In 1952, Harley picked up the glove and introduced its side-valve powered K Model Sport. This bike's performance would reach its full potential five years later, with the installation of overhead valves.

It would then be known as the Sportster, and would go on to be the longest running motorcycle model in the world. Harley's 50th Anniversary was celebrated with a new logo, the V-over-bar design, and coincided with the demise of its last domestic competitor, Indian. During this decade government programs were building new highways, tunnels, expressways and bridges, encouraging people to leave the cities and journey into the country. The Eisenhower administration's development of the Interstate Highway System for the movement of missiles and war materials had the unintended consequence of getting people and their money on the road, much to Harley's delight. In 1958, the Duo-Glide big twin made its appearance, and the advertising phrase "You Meet the Nicest People on a Honda" would prompt Harley to produce the Topper scooter. These were economically robust times, and imported machines from Italy and Germany were taking their share of the American youth market. In 1960, Harley purchased half interest in Aeronatica-Macchi, and used this company's expertise in small bike production and manufacture. By 1967, all of Harley's lightweights were Italian-made, leaving the domestic plants for Electra Glides and Servi-Cars. In 1961, the Sprint was introduced, and

Harley purchased 60% of Tomahawk Boat Manufacturing Company for making fiberglass components. In 1965, the Duo-Glide gave way to the Electra Glide with its new electric starter, a feature that the Sportster line would also receive. The Shovelhead replaced the Panhead, and Cal Rayborn went on to win several victories at Daytona on a KR750. With a decline in financials at the end of the year, Harley merged with American Machine and Foundary, a leisure-time product producer. While this marriage was not a good one, several interesting motorcycles were produced during the decade. In response to the customizing fad of raked frames, little or no fenders, and impossibly high handle bars, Harley introduced a bike with the sporty front end of the X bikes and the big mill of the touring FL, and named it the FX 1200 Super Glide. In a similar vein, the FXS Low Rider, the Cafe Racer, and the FXEF Fat Bob were brought to the market place. The idea of putting out a range of products with similar engines but different body styles had arrived, though the automotive industry had used it for decades. Harley also introduced a more powerful and reliable XR750, a bike that dominated racing for the next thirty years. The merger with AMF was contentious, and tooling problems and the oil crises left the company poorer at the end of the decade.

To reduce overhead, its share of Aero Macchi was sold off, along with its interest and production of light weight bikes. At this stage, Harley's products were viewed as unreliable maintenance nightmares; its market share had dropped to 4% of domestic sales. Quality control had gone out the window, along with its products. In 1981, a group of Harley executives purchased the company back from AMF, and with the motto "The eagle soars alone" moved into a new era. Confident with a rededication to the founders' original precepts of superior quality and superior product, the new management team started to move in that direction. In 1982, a new Sportster was introduced as the FXR/FXRS Super Glide II. The bike featured the FLT's vibration dampening rubber-isolated drive train, a five-speed gearbox,

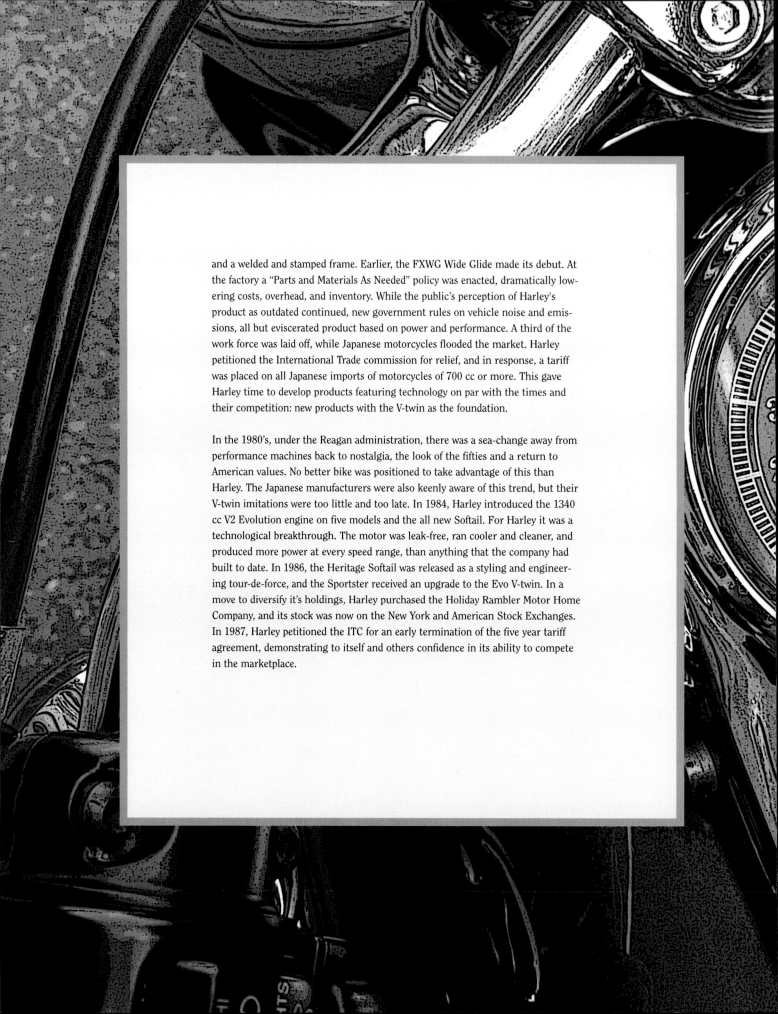

and a welded and stamped frame. Earlier, the FXWG Wide Glide made its debut. At the factory a "Parts and Materials As Needed" policy was enacted, dramatically lowering costs, overhead, and inventory. While the public's perception of Harley's product as outdated continued, new government rules on vehicle noise and emissions, all but eviscerated product based on power and performance. A third of the work force was laid off, while Japanese motorcycles flooded the market. Harley petitioned the International Trade commission for relief, and in response, a tariff was placed on all Japanese imports of motorcycles of 700 cc or more. This gave Harley time to develop products featuring technology on par with the times and their competition: new products with the V-twin as the foundation.

In the 1980's, under the Reagan administration, there was a sea-change away from performance machines back to nostalgia, the look of the fifties and a return to American values. No better bike was positioned to take advantage of this than Harley. The Japanese manufacturers were also keenly aware of this trend, but their V-twin imitations were too little and too late. In 1984, Harley introduced the 1340 cc V2 Evolution engine on five models and the all new Softail. For Harley it was a technological breakthrough. The motor was leak-free, ran cooler and cleaner, and produced more power at every speed range, than anything that the company had built to date. In 1986, the Heritage Softail was released as a styling and engineering tour-de-force, and the Sportster received an upgrade to the Evo V-twin. In a move to diversify it's holdings, Harley purchased the Holiday Rambler Motor Home Company, and its stock was now on the New York and American Stock Exchanges. In 1987, Harley petitioned the ITC for an early termination of the five year tariff agreement, demonstrating to itself and others confidence in its ability to compete in the marketplace.

In 1988, the FXSTS Springer Softail and Sportster 1200 were debuted. Many said that the introduction of the Evo big V-twin was what put Harley back on its feet, while others maintained that innovation and development of new products did it; in any case, Wall Street took notice and its stock responded favorably. The foundation of the Harley Owners Group (H.O.G.) was a success, boasting a worldwide membership of 400,000. In the 1990's, the FLSTF Fat Boy became an instant classic together with the FXDB Dyna Glide Sturgis, the FLHR Road King, and the 30th Anniversary Ultra Classic Electra Glide. In 1993, Harley buys first part, and later all, of the Buell Motor Company, which used the Harley XC883 and 1200 engines as a base for its models. In 1994, Harley's liquid-cooled, dual overhead cam VR1000 enters the Superbike racing arena. The 90's also saw the opening of state-of-the-art manufacturing plants and facilities, from the Midwest US to Brazil. In 1999 the new twin-cam 88 motor was featured on the Touring and Dyna models. The new century saw new products in the Harley show rooms. The FXSTD Softail Deuce and the VRSCA V-Rod were exciting additions, and Buell introduced the single cylinder Blast to excellent reviews, along with the Firebolt XB9R and the XB9S Lightning.


The year 2003 marked Harley's 100th Anniversary. We can be sure that the founders' business plan did not feature a birth-death-and-rebirth scenario for their company… it's been one hell of a ride.

## Chapter One:
## Original Miles...

**1913 Model 9B Single**

1913 was the first year for this F-head single. Similarly, it was the first year for the Harley Racing Department, the Model G Delivery Van and the V-Twin, 1000cc engine. By any measure the early single cylinder gas engines were anemic, but Harley-Davidson offset this inefficiency with a more solidly built, reliable and more comfortable motorcyle—one that was capable of operating over the then most primitive roads and difficult conditions. The Model 9 featured a Bosch Magneto ignition and the vertical fins on the cylinder heads, made for more efficient cooling of the 564cc engine. Prior to 1909 Harley had manufactured its own carburators but now found it easier to outfit it's machine with Schebler float-feed units. A new sprung seat mounted on the sturdy tubular frame made the going easier as well. Mechanical inlet valves and chain drive were welcome features.

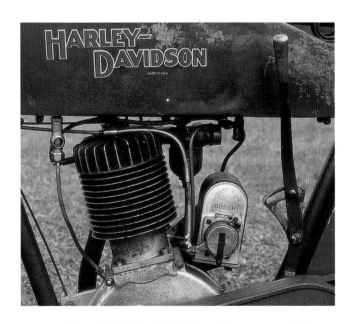

*Left:*

*The bike's single cylinder engine, transmission and carburator all nestled in the loop frame that curved underneath. This all provided better weight distribution and a more stable ride.*

*Opposite page:*

*Harley had become a major motorcycle manufacturer and this rugged reliable machine helped make Harley's fortune.*

# *The Trademark V-Twin Engine was Born...*

**1915 Model 11F**

Harley-Davidson's trademark V-twin engine was born in 1907, when two single cylinders were joined to a common crank-shaft to produce more power. From 1915 on, the V-twin would see constant refinements, but its basic form for the next ninety years would remain unchanged. The 1915 model-year saw a few innovations applied to the Model F, including a three-speed gear box for better performance on grades, and a mechanical oil pump for better lubrication and increased engine life. There were twelve V-twin models listed that year, with either single or three-speed transmissions, and offered with or without an electrical system. Police departments, postal workers and linemen for the utilities, set store in their Harleys for their reliability and performance. With each passing year, the motorcycle became a more and more practical means of transportation.

*Above:*
*A well worn, weathered, but much loved Model 11F.*

*Left:*
*In 1915 an F-head set a speed record of 89.11 mph on a board track.*

*Above:*
The 1915 Model saw many mechanical
improvements, which boosted power and
improved lubrication.

# Crooks Loved Them...

## 1924 Model 24 JDCA

The 1920's were a financially mercurial period for everyone, including Harley-Davidson, and 1924 found the factory running at only 50% capacity. Orders from overseas dealers, domestic commercial orders from businesses, and police departments across the country kept the company in the black. The year 1924 was the first and only year for the Model JDCA. In 1921 Harley had created the Model JD by increasing the cubic inches of the V-twin from 1000 cc to 1213 cc, making it the fastest bike on the road. Crooks loved them, and so did the police. From 1923 to 1930, the JD single shaft model outsold all others in the Harley stable by three to one. The Model 24 JDCA had an F-head V-twin, with 1213 cc of displacement, a three-speed transmission, an electrical system, and aluminum pistons—a new addition for that year.

**Opposite Page:**

*In 1922, Harley created the JD model line of F-head twins by increasing the engine's capacity to 1213cc. In doing so, they created very fast, high performance machines.*

**Right:**

*Harley's patented sprung seat post provided more comfort for the rider.*

*Carrying Bootlegged Coal was*
*One Use for a Sidecar...*

### 1932 VL with Sidecar

In 1930 the F-head V-twin was replaced by the side-valve V-twin in order to create a new, more powerful machine. The motorcycle had several other new features as well, including forged I-beam front forks, a duplex primary chain drive to the rear wheel, a steering head lock, drop-center wheel rims for modern beaded tires, and a horn mounted on a canister-shaped tool box. Though the V-series would prove to be a bestseller in the 1930's, it did suffer from some initial mechanical problems, including those involving, but not limited to, the flywheel, clutch, starter, pistons and valves. The Harley dealerships provided the bike owners with repairs free of charge, but this did little for the lines or Harley's reputation. Twelve versions of the side-valve twin were offered that year, including a sidecar equipped version, shown, and a Servi-Car Model. The letters VL denoted a high compression motor. This totally original machine has had nothing added or removed in over 70 years. The one unusual feature is that this 1932 bike had 1934 fenders when purchased by its original owner. Purchased in 2000 by the current owner, it now serves for recreation and shows.

***Right:***
*The small domed running lights are a very rare feature.*

*This page:*
The sidecar's frame
and skin are all metal.

**Above:**
The 1947 Knucklehead was heavier and faster than it's rival, the Indian, but after eleven years the model saw its final year.

# The Last of the Line...

### 1947 Model 47 FS

The Knucklehead motorcycle was born in 1936. Four things made the Knucklehead unique: increased power due to overhead valves; a single-cam shaft, which was easier to manufacture and maintain; a re-circulating oil system to prevent wasteful burn-off during ignition; and its chrome rocker covers, which would become a visual signature. The Knucklehead's styling cues were added by the renowned industrial designer, Raymond Lowey and automotive design genius Brooke Stevens. Their streamlined efforts showed in the tool box design, air filter, speed-tuned exhaust, cat's-eye instrument panel, chrome Ball-and-Feather Harley-Davidson tank badge, horn, and headlamp. A smooth cowhide saddle and 16-inch wheels improved the ride. The Model 47FS was an overhead valve V-twin with a 1213 cc engine and a four speed transmission. Power output was 48bhp at 5,000 rpm. It was a heavy bike at 535 pounds, and quick with a top speed of over 100 mph. The Knucklehead's mechanical and design changes were evolutionary, and the 1947 model was by and large the same as the 1941 with few changes. After an 11-year run, it was the bike's last year of production. It was also the first year that Harley began to sell its official classic black leather jacket.

*Below:*
*The 1947 Harley was essentially the 1941 model with additions, which included chrome details now available after the war. The brass kick starter is the owner's touch.*

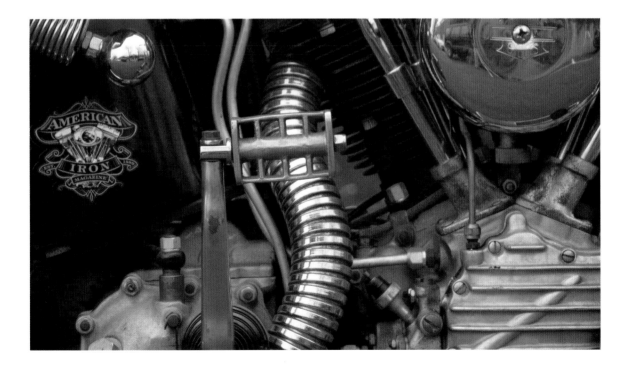

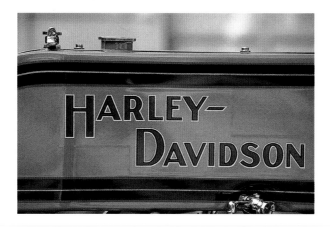

*Above left:*

*Horizontal and vertical cooling fins on the head prevented over-heating.*

*Center left:*

*The tank had two reservoirs: one for gas, and one for oil.*

*Below left:*

*Over time, the Harley logo went through many changes. This is an early example.*

*Opposite page:*

*Lacking a gear box, the machine requires a belt final-drive and rear hub clutch.*

### 1912 Model X8A Silent Gray Fellow

The work force had doubled at Harley-Davidson in the nine years since it had opened its doors. By now, Engineering and Development had realized that an increase in cubic inches was the road to success, and that the motorcycle—due largely to improved design, materials, and manufacturing techniques—had achieved a new level of comfort, convenience, and reliability, evolving into a viable form of transportation. The Model X8 had several interesting features; the 494 cubic centimeter (cc) engine was now attached to a newly designed and strengthened tubular loop frame. Positioned lower on the machine, it provided better balance and superior weight distribution. The X8 had a lower saddle, a belt-drive with final chain drive transmission, a rear hub clutch, and magneto ignition. It lacked both starter and gear box, so the rider had to pedal to start the motor, but the wide and ample handlebars with a twist-grip throttle made this machine all the more manageable. Weighing in at 195 pounds, the motor produced 6.5 brake horsepower (bhp) at 2700 revolutions per minute (rpm). It had a top speed of 45 mph, and could all be yours for $200. Its nickname, "Silent Grey Fellow," stemmed from the bond between this dependable machine and its rider. The model line continued in production until 1918.

# The Sporty Best Seller for The Jazz Age...

### 1920 Model 20J

By 1920, both automobile manufacturers and motorcycle companies were vying for their share and dominance of the market. Despite this, Harley-Davidson—with 2,000 dealers in 67 countries—was the largest bike manufacturer in the world, ahead of Indian and Excelsior. As the year's best seller, the Model J featured a 1000 cc F-Head engine, a three-speed transmission with hand shifter, and a tubular frame with leading fork suspension. Weighing in at 365 pounds, the motorcycle sported a headlight, horn, and speedometer. The fine example shown here is clad in fresh olive-green paint and pin striping. At $395, this powerful machine was capable of speeds of 60 mph. First appearing in 1916, the venerable V-twin still lacked quality metal cylinders; 100 mile teardowns and inspections were suggested by the manufacturer. Harley was now selling 35,000 units annually, topping Indian's 30,000. The year 1920, was also the first year that the Harley racing team completed its victory lap with a pet pig in tow, giving rise to the "Hog" tradition.

**Above:**
*A new electric system and headlight, together with widened handlebars, made the journey more enjoyable.*

**Right:**
*Thanks to Harley's larger V-twin motor, pedaling wasn't required after 1914.*

### 1934 Model 34 VDL with Sidecar

Mechanical problems plagued the V-series from the start. Aluminum engine pistons had to be replaced with those of magnesium alloy, a new oil pump was installed to provide all-important lubrication to the side-valve engine, and a better grade of steel was used to strengthen the frame and forks. All the issues were addressed and corrected. At Harley-Davidson during the height of the Depression, both staff and management were working at reduced pay. The motorcycles themselves saw Art Deco styling touches, rather the technological advances applied to the line. The fenders received curves, the exhaust pipes were swept up and the taillights became streamlined. A new, broad bucket seat was installed and an angular bird motif rested on the gas tank. New two-tone paint schemes were offered to add color to an otherwise drab landscape.

*Above:*
*Chromed fittings reflected the Art Deco style seen here on the horn-cover and fender light.*

*Right:*
*Mechanical improvements offered reliability to H-D customers.*

***Above:***
*The '34 model sported curvaceous new
fenders and an airflow taillight.*

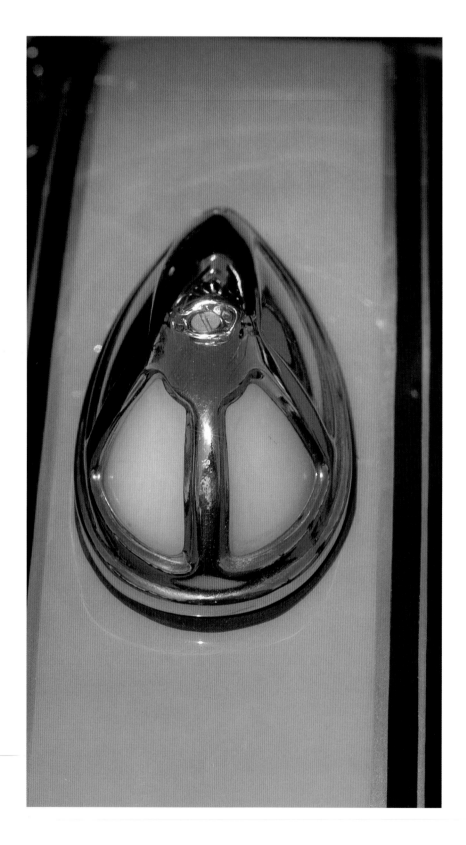

**Left:**
*The chromed Art Deco running light on the front fender was a characteristic feature of the time. Heavy-duty front forks were introduced on the V-series and gave a better ride.*

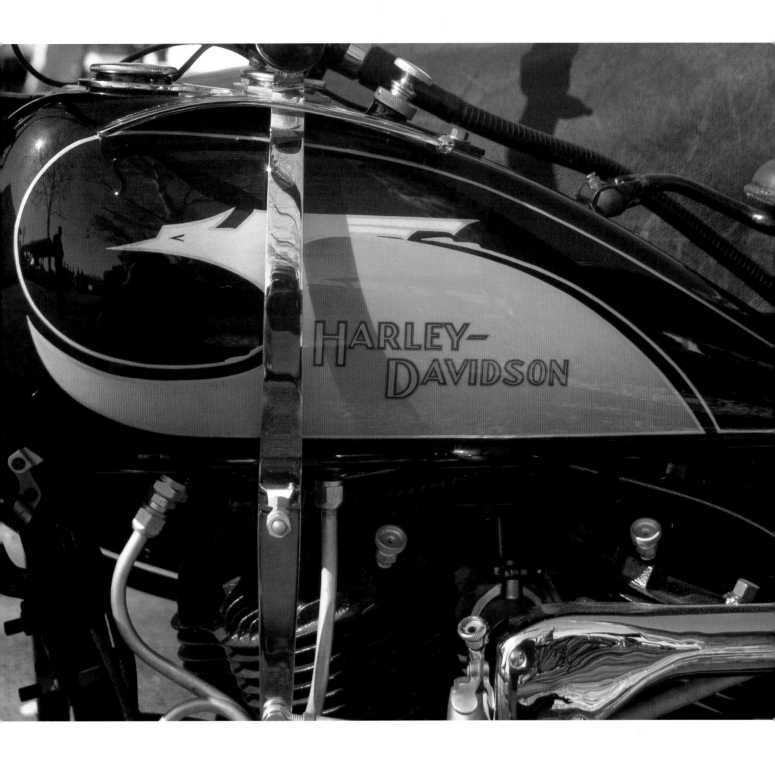

***Above:***
*The bird-motif tank design was a standout. The orange, gold, and black color combination was one of five color schemes that were available.*

## The Honeymoon Special . . .

### 1936 Model 36 VLH

1936 marked the last year for the Flathead V-twins. These machines came with either a 1213cc or 1312cc motor, the latter continuing in service until the mid-1970's on the Servi Cars. The side valve twins had three speeds and a nine-bolt cylinder head, with more performance and larger cooling fins. A special four-speed transmission was also made available by special order. Cosmetic changes were offered with a chrome plated air inlet, a tubular rear wheel stand, and the Bullett and Circle logo. This nicely restored machine was purchased in 1936 for $375 by a young, newly married couple from Tennessee who used it on their honeymoon adventures and as their daily ride. Six decades later, their grandson completed a six-year restoration and produced an award-winning American icon. But back in 1936 there would be another name on the Harley-Davidson "model year lineup": the Knucklehead, which would prove to be the best Harley yet. Featuring a 1000cc overhead valve engine, it was a great seller in its first year.

**Above:**

*This fast Harley was a favorite with the police. Note the fender-mounted sign, the dual pursuit lights, and the fire extinguisher over the siren. All authentic details of a tubulent time.*

A Bike for the
Men-in-Blue...

### 1940 Model 40EL Police

With World War II around the corner, Harley deemed that evolutionary changes and subtle improvements to its line of existing products seemed prudent. Some of the year's changes included a new valve for the reserve fuel tank, the installation of semi-circular foot boards to replace the rectangular model, a cast tear-drop tank emblem, and a cast metal brake drum on the front wheel to reduce road noise. The timing case had ribs cast into its face to provide more efficient cooling to the parts, and the Linkert carburetors had their ports enlarged for better performance. This motorcycle features a 1000cc stock engine and was completely restored by Ken Smith of Philadelphia, Pennsylvania when purchased in 2003. This big twin was Harley's best seller in 1940.

# It was "Swap-Meets and the Web" for Parts...

**1947 FLs / Gray and Cruiser Green**

The 1947 Model FL was for all intents and purposes the same as the 1941 model. It featured an overhead-valve 1200cc motor with a four-speed transmission. Factory trim accessories were now available and chrome was everywhere: on mudguards, fender tips, fuel filler caps, engine covers, horns and wheels. A tank-mounted instrument panel featured a new speedometer face with larger numerals. Mechanical improvements featured the addition of a hydraulic dampener on the front fork to improve the ride. Paint color options for that year included Skyway Blue, Cruiser Green, Brilliant Black, and Flight Red. Even with a 33% jump in price, this model's sales constituted over half of Harley's production for that year. The bike on the preceeding page was purchased by the owner's wife as a bucket-o-parts and was restored over one-and-a-half years. New "old stock" parts and items secured at swap meets aided in the process of rebuilding the motorcycle to original factory specs. We are told that "it runs as good as it looks".

*Left:*
*This 1947 "bobber" is painted in police gray. The rocket-fin exhaust was a popular addition, reflecting the public's interest in aviation and science fiction at that time.*

**Above:**

*This '47 bike is splendid in its gorgeous cruiser-green color scheme. On the technical side, a new electric terminal was installed to accommodate the spotlight.*

**Left:**

*The shift-gate pattern was modified in 1947, with the first gear now positioned in the rear.*

## Chapter Three:
## Racers...

### 1926 Model 26B Racer

For the first time since the end of World War I, single cylinder motorcycles were being offered by Harley-Davidson in Models A, AA, B and BA, available in side-valve or overhead-valve engine configurations. While racing was not a top priority at Harley, the adage "Race on Sunday—sell bikes on Monday" was known and appreciated in the boardroom. Harley victories included Walter Davidson's win in the 1909 Long Island Reliability Run, the 300-mile Independence Day Race at Dodge City in 1915 and all eight National Championship races of 1922. Joe Petrali began racing for Harley in 1925, and ten years later won 13 rounds of the US Dirt Track Championship. Priced $100 lower than their twin cylinder models, the racers featured 346cc of displacement, dropped handle bars and sometimes an unsprung leather seat, a lighter weight and shortened frame, a cut-down rear mud guard, no front fender, paddle foot rests, and knobby treaded tires for better traction: all for $235. This octogenarian carries a racing badge with it's year of manufacture.

*Above:*
*With its shorter frame and dropped handlebars, the 1926 Racer was produced in limited numbers. It competed domestically and abroad.*

*Right:*
*Gas and oil filler caps, lube pump, and gear lever form a neat grouping.*

*Above:*
Harley's teardrop gas tank and chain drive
cover are all finished in stock green.

## *Smaller was Better...*

**1940 Model 40 WLDR**

Introduced in 1927, the "45s" were Harley-Davidson's answer to Indian's 738 cc Flat Head V-twin side valve engines. In 1937, Harley introduced its W-series of sport bikes with this small motor. These bikes stood in marked contrast to the big 1000 cc V-twins that it had built its reputation on. There were three model designations for this line; the W was basic; the WLD was high compression, and the WLDR was the competition variant. The motorcycles featured three-speed chain drive transmission, a tubular cradle frame, and 25 bhp at redline. At 692 pounds, the standard version had a top speed of 96 mph. The lack of rear suspension was compensated for with a larger saddle. The "45s" were basic and hardy, which made their conversion to military use an easy one. The superior quality control, manufacturing, and reliability of this series soon eclipsed its rivals at Indian and Excelsior, and the model continued in production until 1952. This bike is owned by the American racing legend Al Knapp. The bike was rebuilt in the 1980's and is a fine example of the line.

*Right:*
*The W's were introduced in the 1930's, in response to Indian's small 45s.*

**Above:**
*For racing, the mudguards, headlight,
and toolbox have been removed.*

51

***Above:***

*The racers' engines featured racing camshafts, altered cylinder heads, new bearings, bigger valves and reshaped ports.*

**1953 Model 53 KR750 Dirt Track Racer**

There were five K-Series motorcycle models; the Model-K street bike; the Model KK de-tuned racer and street bike; the KR dirt track racer; the KRTT track racer and the KRM desert racer variant. At a glance most of the models looked alike. This line of middle-weights was developed to counter the sportier British 500 cc and 650 cc twins that had found favor in the U.S. after the war. The Model KR featured a 750 cc motor, a four-speed transmission with foot shift and hand clutch, telescopic forks front suspension and a rigid racing frame. The 45° V-twin was, of course, highly tuned for racing. Because the original motor seemed anemic, it's displacement was increased in 1954 to 883 cc, and redesignated the KH. This rare and well preserved all-original example was purchased in a complete state of repair. The #95 was Fred Nix personal number when he rode for Harley and is the bike owners tribute to this individual.

*Above:*
*The KBs used larger fuel tanks for long distance competition.*

*Right:*
*The wide handlebars denote a dirt track racing machine.*

*Just What the Doctor Ordered...*

### 1984 Model 84 XR1000

*Opposite page:*

*The new Blockhead motor was introduced in 1984, and its 997cc on a small frame delivered a lot of performance in a small package.*

*Above:*

*The high-angled dual exhaust-rare on street bikes, added to the performance and enhanced the style.*

In 1983 Harley-Davidson offered the public a limited edition competition dirt track XR750 that could be ridden on the street. To do this, they took the alloy heads and twin carburetors of the 750 and mated them to the bottom half of the XL1000, fitting it all into an XLX frame. It was the fastest production bike Harley had ever produced; some call it their best bike, period. Unfortunately, perception is everything, and the 1000's appearance closely resembled the least expensive model in the Harley product line, but cost significantly more, and sales suffered. Some other features were a classic Sportster fuel tank, 16-inch alloy wheels in the rear, 19-inch wheels in front, high level trumpet dual exhausts, and a speedometer with rev counter on the handlebars. At 470 pounds, it had a top speed of 120 mph. High performance in a small package: just what the doctor ordered.

### 1946-1947 Knuckleheads

This was the last year for the Knucklehead motors' eleven-year run. The motorcycle's most significant physical and mechanical features were the shape of it's rocker covers, its overhead valve configuration that produced more power, the use of a single cam-shaft for the V-twin, and lastly, a dual-stage dry sump lubrication system that recirculated the oil in the engine rather then burning it off through ignition with the fuel. When the Knuckle was first introduced in 1936, its speed and style were something that the public had not seen, and it helped revive Harley's fortunes. The 1947 model line included both high and low compression motors and side-valve or over-head valve configurations. This motorcycle has a stock 1000cc engine, and was restored when the current owner purchased it eleven years ago. Some of its after-market accessories include the saddle bags.

*Above:*
*Big and powerful in its day, this 1946 Knucklehead still weighs less then today's Softail. It has been ridden daily for the last twenty years*

*Opposite page:*
*Originally purchased as a 1947 Knucklehead EL, this bike has seen sixty years of honest wear.*

# A Custom Part From the 50s Sets the Tone...

***Above:***
*A true appreciation for Harley products comes
from using one in a northern winter, running
behind a snowplow.*

### 1948 / 1949 / 1960 Chopper

Vermont is a four-season state with a six month winter. No matter, this is someone's daily ride. The machines creator started with a 1948 Springer front fork, grafted it to a 1949 EL frame, and mounted a stock 1960 Panhead motor with 1200 cc of displacement.

The electrical system was six-volt converted to twelve-volt. It carries dual shotgun exhaust pipes. The handlebars are "dog bone risers," custom additions from the 50's, while the front and rear fenders come from a 1948 FL. The instrument panel carries a Taiwanese reproduction of a 40's speedometer. The transmission and clutch are four-speed, from a 1952 Harley. The wheels and tires are from the 1940's, and the seat is an after-market LaPera. Now, under its second owner, the bike has proven to be fast, cheap, and reliable. For a machine with parts made from sheet metal and scrap iron, that's a great ride.

*This page:*
*A unique one-of-a-kind machine has been fashioned out of an interesting amalgam of parts. Harley equipment and after-market products have been combined to make a road-worthy and street-legal machine.*

***Above:***

*The electric starting system brought a new era to motorcycling. Introduced a year earlier on the Servi Car, this feature was first offered to consumers on the Electra Glide.*

### 1965 Model 65 FLB Electra Glide

With its debut in 1965, the Electra Glide was the last in the line of Panhead-powered machines. Its predecessors included the Hydra Glide of 1949 and the Duo Glide of 1958. Electric starters on the Japanese Hondas forced Harley-Davidson to use them on their 1200 cc machine. Developed the year before on the Model G Servi-Cars, it proved sound enough to be used as a feature on the FLB. Adding an electric starter to the motorcycle required other modifications, including a larger twelve-volt battery, a beefed-up twelve-volt electric system, and a new starter assembly to handle the torque. The specifications for the Electra Glide included an OHV V-twin motor of 1200 cc that produced 60 bhp at 5400 rpm, a four-speed hand shifter, tubular steel cradle, hydraulically dampened telescopic front forks, a rear swing-arm, larger oil tank and fuel tank, a foot shifter on the FLHB model, and new cast-aluminum primary drive covers bolted to the transmission. It's a big bike at 783 pounds, and it is what most consider to be the classic American touring machine.

*Above:*

*While this motorcycle is spare and spartan in appearance, the coming years would see, more and more accessories added to the FL models.*

*Overleaf:*

*The new cast aluminum primary is seen below the chromed air filter cover. The kick starter was retained despite the addition of the new electric starter.*

# *The Big, Big Classic...*

### 2005 Model 05 FLHTC / FLHTCI

The great symbol of American touring bikes, the Electra Glide Ultra Classic, was introduced in 1989 as part of the FLT/Tour Glide family. The model has used all of Harley's most famous motors, including the Shovelhead, Panhead, Evo and now the rubber-mounted twin-cam "88" with 1450cc.

In 1964, the first Electra Glide debuted Harley's electric starter, and beefier 12-volt electric system. But any real discussion of this model must center around the accessories, since it carries features and amenities not found on less expensive rides; twin spotlights, running lights, a CD player, an intercom with a helmet-mounted headset, cruise control, fuel injection, AM/FM stereo, four speakers, weather band, citizen band, and an air suspension system in the front and rear that can vary the height depending on the load and road conditions. The model reflects a steady curve of refinements over the last 30-plus years. Someone said of the Electra Glide experience, "If the wind wasn't blowing it would be like sitting in my living room". Fully loaded with two, the bike weighs almost a half-ton. Go in comfort, arrive in style.

**Above:**
*Digital read-outs, an intercom and a host of accessories make the Ultra Classic a great cruiser.*

**Above:**
*The logo inscribed on the gear box cover is the owner's tribute to his professional as a fire captain and to the lost firefighters of 9/11.*

***Above:***
*This is a "Full Dresser" on the famous FLT chassis; capable of eating up the miles in comfort.*

Chapter Five:
Customs...

# One Man's Tribute to a Valued Machine...

### 1913 Model 9B Silent Grey Fellow Custom

The year 1913 saw continued mechanical improvements to the Harley-Davidson product line. A chain now replaced the leather belt drive which had, up until then, provided quiet but unreliable power to the rear wheel. Larger cylinders and new inlet valves gave more horsepower and better performance. Even though the competition–the automobile–was becoming more affordable, Harley's sales continued to improve. Five models were now offered in the 1913 line up.

This award-winning restoration by master-craftsman Bill Eggers, took one year to complete, and started with the motor, frame, handlebars, and wheels. Approximately half of the parts are old and half are new, or newly fabricated. Antique swap meets, the world wide web, motorcycle clubs and enthusiast magazines were all good sources for finding and purchasing parts. While not entirely authentic, the graphics on the motorcycle's tank is a tribute to the company's 90th anniversary. The original Harley work shed is seen on the left panel, and a rendering of Harley's first motorcycle, the 1903 Serial #1, is on the right.

***Opposite:***
*The machine shown here was a basket case in 1985, and its one-year restoration started with a new motor and frame, put together with missing parts from antique motorcycle meets, flea markets, and auctions.*

***Above:***
*For illumination, acetylene gas is fed from the tank to the front and rear lamps.*

# *Wild Bill's Labor of Love...*

## 1953 Model 53G Servi-Car

"50 Years American Made." In 1953, with these words emblazoned across their new logo, Harley-Davidson celebrated its anniversary. It was also noteworthy that Indian Motorcycle Company closed its doors for good that year, making Harley the preeminent motorcycle manufacturer in the U.S.. The year 1932 was the first for the three-wheeled Model G Servi-Car, and from there it had a remarkable production run, up to and including the last disc-brake equipped models in 1973. Virtually unchanged from the W-series, the model was generally popular with police departments and small businesses. Geared for low-speed use in traffic and on parking patrols, they were very user-friendly; its three-wheeled stance provided stability, while its cargo box's internal capacity made it perfect for commercial applications. Powered by a Flat Head side valve V-twin engine with 738cc displacement, it had three forward gears and one reverse, and its tubular cradle had an additional sub-frame to accommodate the box extension. In 1967 the box's wood and metal construction was replaced with a fiberglass product. Some of the machine's other features included wing mirrors to aid in backing up and telescoping front forks like the big twins of the time. The police variants featured a dynamo-operated siren, chrome headlight pack, lever operated siren on the grip, red police lights and yellow indicators along with an adjustable-height windshield, and the whole improved with a nice dash of chrome trim. The three-wheeler weighed in at 598 pounds, and its internal capacity could add another 500 pounds to the total.

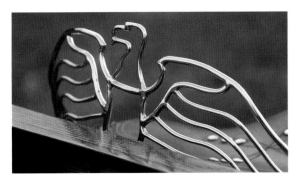

**Opposite page:**
*Originally a police bike, the handgrip functions on the handlebars are reversed. The gas here is on the left, freeing the rider's right hand.*

**Above:**
*The eagle seatback design was fashioned from a quarter-inch rod.*

**Right:**
*The Servi-Car box is made of white oak with walnut inlays. The frame and transmission were extended by 18 inches to accommodate this addition. This bike is another Bill Eggers creation.*

*Extras are What Make the Ride Special...*

### 1971 Model 71 FLH

In 1971, American Machine and Foundary had taken over Harley-Davidson, and the Honda CB750 was the machine to beat if not emulate in terms of product performance and reliability. It was also the year that Harley introduced the FX Super Glide, its first "custom" bike. The Duo Glide Model FLH was first released in 1958 when big twin cruisers were popular.

At the time, comfort and dependability were key, but accessories were what made the motorcycle more than just transportation. Chrome was everywhere. On luggage racks, exhausts, instrument covers, air filters, grab handles, bars and rails, valve covers, horns, headlamps...you get the idea. The list was endless, as were the colors available. The Model 71 FLH had an OHV V-twin 1213cc engine, four-speed hand shift transmission, tubular cradle, and hydraulically dampened telescopic front forks. It produced 55 bhp at 7200 rpms, and weighed 670 pounds with a top speed of 100 mph. About 5475 were built that year.

**Opposite page:**
*Purchased in 1975 and remodeled in 1980, this motorcycle carries the owner's, once again Bill Eggers, unique touches.*

**Above:**
*The stirrups were removed from the saddle after a mishap with a New York City taxi.*

**Left:**
*The American Flyer logo, eagle, and 'USA' are the owner's personal tributes to his country. The 1200 is a stock fender tip device.*

## 2003 Model FLHTC Electra Glide Ultra Classic

In the 1960's, Honda stirred the public's interest in motorcycles like no other brand before it. In response, Harley released the Electra Glide Classic to compete with other touring bike imports. The model featured a new 12-volt electrical system, an electric starter, a beefier frame, a new oil tank, auto spark advance, and stronger cases and clutch. Harley's intention was to make biking easier and more trouble-free. It was, and remains today, the quintessential American motorcycle. With its King of the Highway equipment, everything on this bike was big: the saddle, headlight, saddlebags, fiberglass luggage rack, air cleaner, and steer horn handle bars. Today's bike features a wider rear tire, a batwing fairing, full instrument complement, stereo and a rubber mounted twin-cam 88 inch OHV engine. It is a luxurious road machine.

*Above:*

*Originally appearing in 1989 the Ultra Classic came with a CB radio and cruise control. This "Full-Dresser" carries over $10,000 in lights and other extras.*

*Opposite page:*

*2003 marked the 100th anniversary of uninterrupted motorcycle production for Harley, an achievement no other company could claim.*

**Above:**

To commemorate the company's 100th birthday, this classic touring bike carried a series of badges and markings on the motor case, air cleaner, and seat.

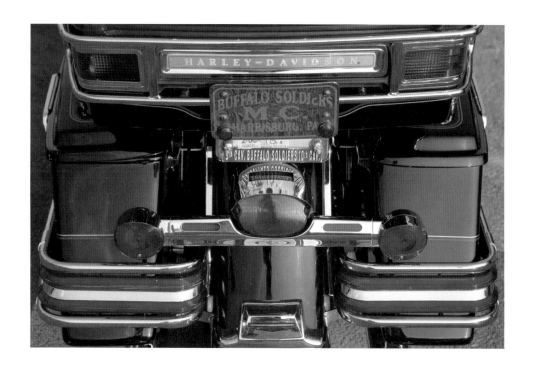

*Above and right:*
Hard saddlebags with
wrap-around reflectors were
an option for touring.

## The Beast's Heart is Liquid-Cooled ...

### 2003 Model 03 VRSCA V-Rod

Harley-Davidson, working in cooperation with Porsche, applied a lot of the technology developed for the VR1000, and in 2001 introduced the VRSCA. The machine looks like nothing that came before it at Harley.

The heart of the beast is a dual overhead cam V-twin set at 60 degrees with 1130cc of displacement; it features liquid cooling, four valves per cylinder, a 115 bhp and 8,500 rpm engine with a five-speed belt drive transmission, a tubular steel "perimeter" frame, telescopic front forks, swing-arm rear suspension, 595 pounds, and a top speed of 130 mph. The engine and gearbox are a single unit, and the stiffer external chassis permits the gas tank to be behind the engine, not over it. New manufacturing methods had to be employed to shape the bike's exoskeletal frame. The motorcycle's suspension is adjustable, and the wheels are milled solid aluminum discs. Finished in space age shades of aluminum, brushed metal, and chrome, the V-rod's performance is beyond that of existing products in the Harley stable.

### 2004 Model 04 CVO FXSTD

For special consideration, the Custom Vehicle Operations (CVO) Division at Harley-Davidson will build a limited edition Softail Deuce. This has a bored and stroked twin-cam 1690 cc motor tuned to Enraged Eagle specifications. Custom touches include slash-cut mufflers, teardrop air box, low profile seat, chopped suspension, 180mm rear and 21-inch front tire, an elongated gas tank, six-spoke custom wheels, and a lot of chrome-plated accessories. AM/FM/CD stereo and special instruments complete the package. This product is an excellent example of how Harley can use one frame and motor and together with a selection of different fuel tanks, wheels, seats and colors to create an endless number of models. The specifications for the standard Harley Softail Deuce, for comparison, are: OHV V-twin engine 1400cc, 69 bhp, five-speed transmission, tubular cradle frame, telescopic front forks, swing-arm rear, and a total weight of 682 pounds.

*Above:*
*Here is the essence of modern motorcycle sophistication, in yellow and chrome.*

*Opposite page:*
*The Vince & Hines big radius exhaust and Kuriakin air cleaner were after-market options.*

*Left:*
Triple-banded grips are
also on the foot-pegs.

*Below:*
The two-tone paint
finish of silver and
chrome yellow is set off
with orange pinstripes.

***Above:***
*Twin rear disc brakes have six piston
calipers and are drilled.*

# Just Fun, Pure and Simple...

### 2005 Model 05 1200/Trike

The Theater of Travel could not have been better served than with the Harley-Davidson Sportster. The bike is meant purely for the sport of travel, and is the least complex way to experience motorcycling. Introduced in 1957 to counter foreign imports that were flooding the markets, and still in production today, it is the longest-lived motorcycle model in the world. Upgrades and improvements over the years have done little to detract from its mission of having fun. This particular motorcycle originally came with an "88" motor, which the owner replaced with a "1200" in 2005. The machine was sent to the Lehman Trike Manufacturing Company in South Dakota for the modification. At $11,000, this nine-day conversion provided an incredibly stable ride for the cyclist and his passenger, with its broad tires and wide stance. The specifications for the Sportser 1200 are: OHV Evolution engine, 66 bhp at 5,200 rpm, five-speed transmission, steel twin cradle frame, and a weight of 491 pounds. In addition to the Sportster accessories package, the owner also added a Cherokee Seat with the back rest and a larger luggage rack (after the photos here were taken).

*Opposite page:*
*For long, straight roads, this is a fine touring bike for two. The Lehman conversion is a simple nine-day affair, and then you're off.*

**Left:**
*The leather tool bag under the light and the windshield were additions–not stock– on the Sportster.*

**2005 Model 05 FLHRCI**

First introduced in 1995 as a middle-weight, middle-distance touring bike, the Road King is an old idea made modern with updates; like a sequential port fuel injection system, a new touring chassis, and a rubber-mounted twin-cam 88 engine with belt drive. Visually, the bike plays off the nostalgia for the fifties, mimicking the look of the Electra Glide with it's big head lamp, windshield, traditional valanced mud guard, spoke wheels, and chrome trim.

Leather hard-bags and whitewall tires distinguish the Road King Classic from the hard panniered Road King. Additional features include a narrower profile and lower center of gravity. That feature, together with the wide handle bars, make for a more comfortable trip. Quieter, with lowered fuel emissions and better fuel economy, it serves for a pleasant ride on winding country roads or on the highway.

*Above:*
*The addition of fuel injection is noted on the chromed air filter cover.*

*Opposite page:*
*The Road King is a great American touring bike. With its traditional looks, economy, lower emissions, and other improvements, it's a new riding experience.*

## The Sportster, it's a Survivor...

### 2005 Model 05 XL1200S

Based on the Model KH, 1957 was the first year for the XL Sportster. A lighter, more nimble version of the big twins it would go on to become the longest surviving motorcycle in the business. Designed as a middle-weight touring bike and one that was competitive with the overseas imports, the engineers at H-D mated a larger cylinder head with a greater bore and stroke to a smaller V-twin to give better performance. Originally fitted with a V-twin OHV of 54 cu.in., the Evo 1200 version was fitted in 1988. This OKV V-twin has 1200cc; 59 bhp; 5-speed; 692 lbs.; 108 mph. Over the years the model has received small, incremental changes in suspension, power and styling. The Sportster line includes the Sportster 1200, Sportster 1200 Sport, Sportster 1200 Custom, Sportster 883, and Sportster 883 Hugger. Recent modifications to the model include a new rubber mounted motor to reduce vibration and road fatigue, a tach, dual front disc brakes, taller suspension and a smaller fuel tank.